A soap timeline

c. 2800 BC

Soap is made in ancient Babylon.

1608

Commercial soapmaking begins in the American colonies.

312 BC

The first Roman public bath supplied with water from aqueducts is built.

1823

French chemist Michel Chevreul works out the process of saponification.

c. 1550 BC

Ancient Egyptians make soap from oils and alkaline salts.

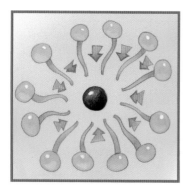

1791

French chemist Nicolas Leblanc patents a cheap method of making soda ash, a soap ingredient.

1200s AD

The English make soap in quantity for commercial sale.

1861

Belgian chemist Ernest Solvay finds an even cheaper method of making soda ash.

1916

The first synthetic detergent is developed in Germany.

1970s–1990s

Arrival of liquid hand soaps, cold-water detergents and gel dishwasher detergents.

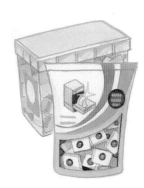

1886

American Josephine Cochrane invents the first automatic dishwasher.

1950s

Dishwasher detergents are developed.

2000s

Arrival of disposable cleaning wipes, dissolvable detergent packets and eco-friendly detergents.

Washing clothes the traditional way

Before washing machines were invented, clothes were washed by hand using several specialised pieces of equipment.

Mangle: *Also known as a wringer, this is a hand-powered device that squeezes water from wet laundry.*

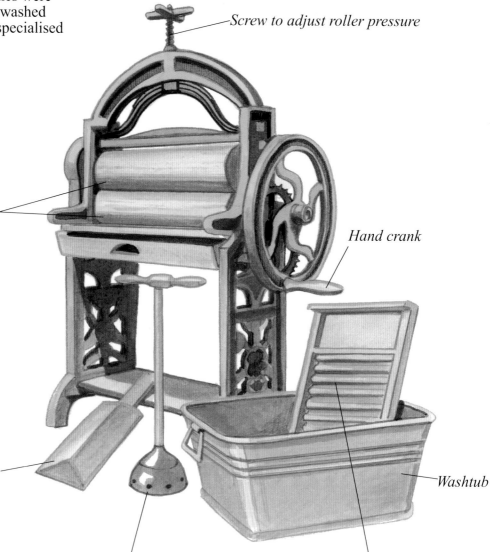

Screw to adjust roller pressure

Rollers

Hand crank

Wooden bat, or **beetle:** *This was used to beat the dirt out of clothing.*

Washtub

Posser, or **washing dolly:** *A pole used for 'possing' or mixing laundry while hand-washing it. The domed end is made of copper.*

Washboard: *A rectangular wooden frame with a series of ridges (made of wood, metal or glass) for clothing to be rubbed on.*

Author:

Alex Woolf studied history at Essex University,
England. He is the author of over 60 books for
children, many of them about history and science.
They include *You Wouldn't Want to Live Without
Books!*, *You Wouldn't Want to Live Without Fire!* and
You Wouldn't Want to Live Without Money!

Artist:

Mark Bergin was born in Hastings in 1961.
He studied at Eastbourne College of Art and has
specialised in historical reconstructions as well as
aviation and maritime subjects since 1983. He lives
in Bexhill-on-Sea with his wife and three children.

Series creator:

David Salariya was born in Dundee,
Scotland. He has illustrated a wide range of books
and has created and designed many new series
for publishers in the UK and overseas. David
established The Salariya Book Company in 1989.
He lives in Brighton with his wife, illustrator
Shirley Willis, and their son Jonathan.

Editor: **Stephen Haynes**

Editorial assistant: **Rob Walker**

Cover artwork: **David Antram**

PAPER FROM
SUSTAINABLE
FORESTS

Published in Great Britain in MMXVI by
Book House, an imprint of
The Salariya Book Company Ltd
25 Marlborough Place, Brighton BN1 1UB
www.salariya.com
www.book-house.co.uk
ISBN: 978-1-910184-95-0

S A L A R I Y A

3 5 7 9 8 6 4 2

A CIP catalogue record for this book is available
from the British Library.

Printed and bound in China.
Reprinted in MMXVII.

Visit
www.salariya.com
for our online catalogue and
free fun stuff.

You Wouldn't Want to Live Without™

Soap!

Written by
Alex Woolf

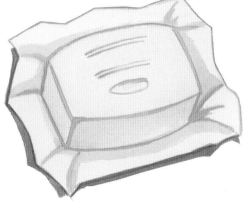

Illustrated by
Mark Bergin

Series created by
David Salariya

BOOK HOUSE
a SALARIYA imprint

Contents

Introduction

When you wash your hands, do you ever think about the soap you're using? Why not just use water to clean yourself? What is the point of soap? How does it help in the cleaning process?

In this book we'll learn all about soap – what it is, how it's made and how it works. We'll look at its history and find out what life was like before soap. We'll also look at the various uses of soap – not just for keeping you clean, but also for washing your family's clothes, dishes, cars, carpets and pets, and other uses that might surprise you. Welcome to the captivating, compelling and very clean world of soap…

WE USE SOAP all the time, but hardly think about it. Yet without it our world would be a very dirty, dangerous place. Our baths might be quicker, but our clothes and bodies would be smellier, and we'd all spend a lot more time being ill because germs would spread much more easily.

What if we didn't have soap?

Imagine a world without soap. We would have to wash ourselves with water alone, and water is not that efficient at cleaning. We would have to learn to live with a lot more dirt in our lives. Germs would spread more easily from person to person, and from our hands to the food we eat, causing more illness. Harmful bacteria would find a home in our clothing, towels, bedclothes and on our less-than-clean kitchen surfaces, dishes, mugs and chopping boards. In short, without soap we'd be a lot less healthy.

Yet soap hasn't always existed. And even after soap was invented, not all civilisations used it. People found other ways to keep clean.

GRUBBY GREEKS. The ancient Greeks bathed, but did not use soap. They cleaned their bodies with blocks of clay, sand, pumice and ashes, then covered themselves with perfumed oil. They scraped off the oil and dirt with a metal implement called a strigil.

Strigil

6

From a ladies' magazine, 1867: 'If you want to have a good head of hair . . . use nothing else to clean it but strong, cold black tea. Rub it into the roots every evening before going to bed.'

SMOKE CLEANING. The Himba people of Namibia don't wash with water, because it's so scarce. Instead, they sit in a room filled with incense smoke until they sweat, then rub themselves with cream and scented ochre to give their bodies a reddish glow.

CLEANING WITH URINE. The Romans cleaned clothing by soaking it in a mixture of urine and water (above). Ammonia in the urine lifted the dirt off the clothing. Urinals were placed on street corners so that urine could be collected for this purpose.

VICTORIAN HAIR WASH. In the 19th century, before the invention of shampoo, people washed their hair in many unusual substances, including lemon juice, black tea, rosemary and egg yolks.

How do germs spread?

To understand why soap is so important, we need to take a look at germs, the microscopic invaders that soap helps us keep under control. Germs are tiny organisms that can get into our bodies and sometimes make us ill. There are four major types: bacteria, viruses, fungi and protozoa. Germs can be spread from person to person through the air in sneezes and coughs, or even by breathing on someone. They can also spread through sweat, saliva and blood. One of the best ways we can prevent germs from spreading is by washing our hands with soap and water. If we do this well and often, we're less likely to catch infections.

A···a···

No, you can't catch a computer virus!

BACTERIA (left) are tiny one-celled creatures that can live in or outside our bodies. Some of them cause infections such as sore throats, ear infections and pneumonia. Not all bacteria are bad; some help us with digestion.

VIRUSES can only grow and reproduce inside living cells. They cause chickenpox, measles, flu and many other diseases.

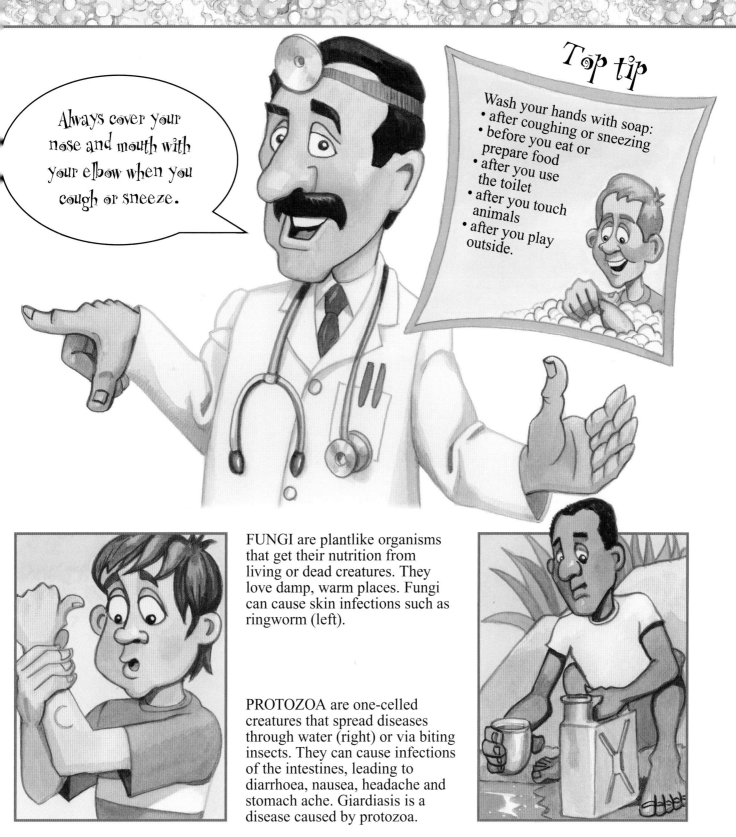

Always cover your nose and mouth with your elbow when you cough or sneeze.

Top tip

Wash your hands with soap:
• after coughing or sneezing
• before you eat or prepare food
• after you use the toilet
• after you touch animals
• after you play outside.

FUNGI are plantlike organisms that get their nutrition from living or dead creatures. They love damp, warm places. Fungi can cause skin infections such as ringworm (left).

PROTOZOA are one-celled creatures that spread diseases through water (right) or via biting insects. They can cause infections of the intestines, leading to diarrhoea, nausea, headache and stomach ache. Giardiasis is a disease caused by protozoa.

What is soap and how does it work?

Soap is a substance made of fatty acids (chemicals found in fats and oils) mixed with an alkali (a chemical that reacts with and neutralises acids). Why does soap clean better than water by itself? Well, most dirt contains oil. Oil and water can't bind together, so washing with water leaves most of the dirt behind. Soap is useful because its molecules are soluble in both oil and water. The soap binds to both the water and the dirt, so when you rinse the soap off, the dirt comes off with it.

1. LOVE–HATE RELATIONSHIP. The head of the soap molecule is hydrophilic (it loves water), so it attaches to water; the molecule's tail is hydrophobic (it hates water) and it binds to the oil in the dirt.

2. MICELLES. When dirt mixes with soapy water, the soap molecules form tiny clusters called micelles. The water-loving heads point outwards, sticking to the water and forming the micelle's outer surface. The water-hating tails stick to the oil, trapping it in the centre.

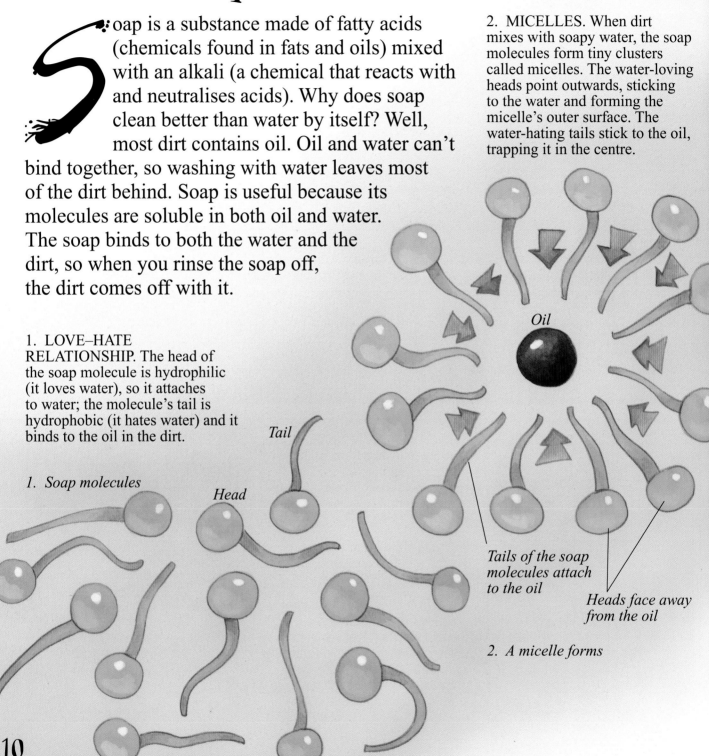

1. Soap molecules

Tail

Head

Oil

Tails of the soap molecules attach to the oil

Heads face away from the oil

2. A micelle forms

You can do it!

Put cooking oil and water in a jar. Screw on the lid and shake. The oil and water separate into layers. Add drops of washing-up liquid. Shake again. This time it's a cloudy mixture: oil and water are no longer in separate layers.

Separate

Mixed

3. The micelle containing the oil and dirt is washed away

3. WASHING AWAY THE DIRT. With the oil trapped in the centre of the micelle, out of contact with the water, soap can do its job. When you wash your hands with soap, dirt mixed with oil from your skin is pulled inside the micelles, then rinsed away.

MAKING WATER WETTER. Water has a property called surface tension, which is what causes it to form into beads on surfaces such as glass and fabric. Soap is a surfactant: it reduces water's surface tension so that it spreads more easily across surfaces. This is often referred to as making the water 'wetter'. The easier spreading makes the water more effective for cleaning.

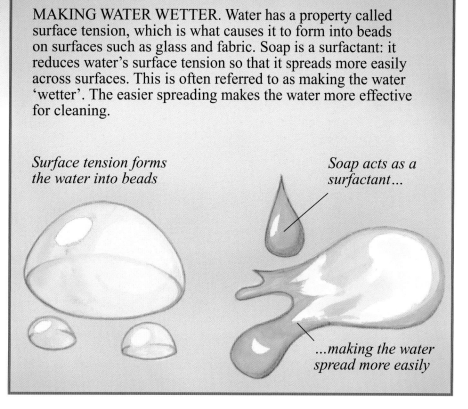

Surface tension forms the water into beads

Soap acts as a surfactant...

...making the water spread more easily

11

When was soap invented?

We don't actually know when soap was invented, but we do know that it's been in use for at least 4,800 years. By 1550 BC, the Egyptians were making soap by mixing fats with alkaline salts. Although the Romans at first didn't use soap, preferring the Greek oil-and-strigil method, they were aware of it. According to 1st-century AD writer Pliny the Elder, the Germans and Gauls used soap, and the men used it more than the women!

BABYLONIAN SOAP. The earliest reference to soapmaking comes from a Babylonian tablet from 2800 BC. It describes a recipe using animal and vegetable fats boiled with ashes.

Animal fat? Ashes? And this is supposed to make you clean?

THE WORD *SOAP*, according to Roman legend, comes from Mount Sapo, a fictional mountain near Rome. Laundrywomen discovered soap when rain washed ashes and animal fat into the River Tiber from sacrifices on the mountaintop.

Top tip

An ancient Egyptian text from c. 2000 BC advises: 'To drive the odour of sweat from the body of a person in summer, take incense, lettuce, fruit of [an unidentified plant], myrrh. Mix. Rub the patient with it.'

Try it!

SOAP SLUMP. By AD 200, the Romans had embraced soap. But when the empire collapsed in 467, so did soap use. The early Church discouraged bathing, believing it a pagan practice. The decline in personal hygiene contributed to the medieval plagues.

It's perfect for that post-battle bath.

A SECRET CRAFT. During the later Middle Ages, soap became a luxury item. Soapmaking guilds guarded their trade secrets closely, adding perfumes to their recipes. The Crusaders developed a taste for 'Aleppo soap', made with olive and laurel oils, and took this from the Middle East back to Spain.

When did soap become popular?

During the late Middle Ages, soap was a luxury product used only by the rich. Bathing was infrequent, because many people believed they could catch diseases from water touching the skin – an idea that originated during the Black Death. Habits started to change from the end of the 18th century. Advances in chemistry, as well as changes in fashion, brought soap use to the masses, and bathing became a regular event for everyone. A big advance in the soapmaking process came in the 1790s with the development of a new method for producing soda ash, a key ingredient of soap.

1791: French chemist Nicolas Leblanc discovers a cheap method of making soda ash from salt. But his factory is confiscated by French revolutionaries.

QUEEN ELIZABETH I (reigned 1558–1603) is said to have remarked: 'I bathe once a month, whether I need it or not.'

1823: French chemist Michel Chevreul works out the process of saponification (see pages 16–17). Fate is much kinder to him: he lives to be 102.

Why didn't I think of that?

1861: Belgian chemist Ernest Solvay discovers an even cheaper way of making soda ash, from ammonia, limestone and salt. Poor old Leblanc's method falls out of use.

How it works

In the American colonies, soap was made in the autumn, when animals were butchered, to make use of the tallow and lard from the carcasses. Ash from the fire and waste cooking grease were also used.

It floats!

You're still fired.

1880s: US manufacturers Procter & Gamble introduce Ivory soap, famous because it floats. Ivory is whipped with air during its production. According to legend, it was invented by accident when a worker left the mixing machine on too long.

BATHING AND HEALTH. From the late 18th century, bathing was promoted as a way of treating illness. Hydrotherapy became popular from the 1820s. The first modern public baths were opened in Liverpool in 1829.

LOUIS PASTEUR developed his 'germ theory' in the 1860s, proving the link between microorganisms and infectious disease. The importance of hygiene and regular bathing became established fact.

15

How is soap made?

What goes into soap

Soap is made by means of a chemical reaction between fats and oils, or their fatty acids, and a water-soluble alkali. This process is known as saponification. For bars of soap, the fats used are mainly beef and mutton tallow, and the oils are mostly palm, coconut and palm-kernel oils. The most commonly used alkalis are sodium hydroxide, also known as caustic soda, and potassium hydroxide, known as caustic potash. These raw ingredients are usually treated to remove impurities before they are mixed together.

Animal fat

Coconut oil

ALKALIS affect the quality of a soap. Soaps made from sodium hydroxide are firm, whereas those made from potassium hydroxide are softer, or often liquid.

Bar of soap

Caustic soda

THE FATS AND OILS used to make soap affect its 'feel'. For example, soap made from olive oil, known as Castile soap, is famously extra-mild. Some soaps, such as Aleppo and Castile soap, are made from plant oils and do not contain animal fat.

SAPONIFICATION. First, the fats, oils and alkali are boiled together in a big kettle. The fats and oils react with the alkali to produce soap, water and a sweet substance called glycerine. The glycerine and any unprocessed fats are removed, and the soap and water are boiled again. The mixture separates into two layers.

Soap

Water

Impurities

NEAT SOAP. The top layer is 'neat soap' (soap and water); the lower layer contains impurities.

Steam

Fats

Oils

You can do it!

To make your own fancy soap,* spray the inside of a plastic mould with cooking spray. Ask an adult to microwave the bar of soap until melted. Add drops of soap dye and stir in. Partly fill the mould with soap. Let it cool for 20 minutes. Pour more soap into the mould. Leave for 2 hours. Once hard, pop the soap out.

NEUTRALISATION. Some soap is made by a different process: the fats and oils are broken down by high-pressure steam to yield fatty acids and glycerine. The fatty acids are then boiled with the alkali to produce neat soap.

Finishing

BLENDING. The lower layer is removed and the neat soap blended with fragrances and dyes.

CUTTING. Once a uniform texture has been achieved, the mixture is cut into bars.

STAMPING. The bars, now cooled and hardened, are stamped into their final shape in a soap press.

How were clothes washed in the past?

For much of history, people washed their clothes in rivers with no soap at all. Wooden bats, or 'beetles', might be used to beat the dirt out of clothing. Wood or stone boards with grooved scrubbing surfaces, called washboards, gradually replaced natural rocks. Where there were no watercourses, laundry was done in vessels of heated water. Boiling water was an effective means of removing dirt. A 'posser' or 'washing dolly' was a pole used to pound and stir laundry while washing it.

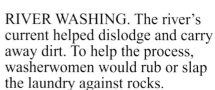

RIVER WASHING. The river's current helped dislodge and carry away dirt. To help the process, washerwomen would rub or slap the laundry against rocks.

BUCKING. Every few months, washerwomen gave linens a more thorough clean by soaking them in lye, an alkali made from wood ashes. The process, called bucking, took a week, but made the linens impressively white.

1. Hot water is poured through ashes spread on bucking cloth.
2. Bucking tub contains laundry.
3. Hole beneath tub lets dissolved lye run out into bucket.
4. Lye is reheated and the process repeated many times.

I'll need a faster river to get these stains out!

Top tip

If the river has frozen, chop a hole in the ice with an axe. Erect a screen to protect yourself from the icy winds. Try not to get frostbite when you swish your dirty linen in the water.

Don't you dare rain!

DRYING AND BLEACHING. After bucking, linens were rinsed, then spread out on the grass or on bushes and dried and bleached in the sunshine.

WASH HOUSES. Laundry was often done in public wash houses. Water from a river was channelled into the building, which had basins for washing and rinsing.

19

How does soap help wash clothes?

During the 1800s, soap became increasingly available as an aid to washing clothes. Many people continued to wash their linen in lye, but used soap for difficult stains. They might make soap at home, using ashes, fat and salt, or the local shop might sell them a piece cut from a large block. By the late 1800s, the first commercially made, ready-wrapped bars of laundry soap were being sold. Detergents followed in 1916. Like soap, detergent is a surfactant – it mixes with both grease and water – but it's made of synthetic rather than natural ingredients.

We'll have to find something to wash with!

DETERGENT first appeared in 1916, developed in Germany due to a shortage of fats for making soap during World War I.

I miss the wash-house gossip, though.

EARLY WASHING MACHINES. The first hand-operated washing machines appeared in the 1800s. Mangles (see opposite page) made the job of drying clothes easier. Now, washing could be done in the home, rather than at the wash house, and it became a weekly ritual.

PROS AND CONS. When soap is used with hard water (which contains dissolved minerals) it tends to cause scum; detergent does not. But detergents contain ingredients that can be harsh on the skin – fine for washing clothes, not so great for washing hands.

BUILDERS AND BLEACHES. After World War II, detergents really took off. Additives called 'builders' made surfactants bind to more grime; bleaches made white clothing look whiter than ever (below).

How it works

Mangles, or wringers, were invented in the United States in the 1800s. When the handle was turned, the rollers compressed the wet clothing and squeezed the excess water out of it.

Sparkle!

Dazzle!

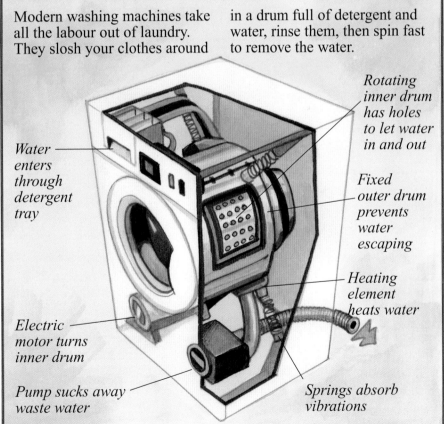

Modern washing machines take all the labour out of laundry. They slosh your clothes around in a drum full of detergent and water, rinse them, then spin fast to remove the water.

Water enters through detergent tray

Rotating inner drum has holes to let water in and out

Fixed outer drum prevents water escaping

Heating element heats water

Electric motor turns inner drum

Pump sucks away waste water

Springs absorb vibrations

21

How does soap help wash dishes?

Until the late Middle Ages, most people would carry their dirty dishes to the river for cleaning, or women would carry water in buckets to their homes. By the 1700s, domestic servants were washing up in stone sinks in a yard behind the kitchen, using cold water from a pump. The servant would shave off flakes of soap from a large bar to use as a surfactant. In the 19th century, new cleaning products emerged, including Bath bricks (early scouring pads) and emery powder for knives and iron utensils, and mild, creamy soaps for tackling greasy dishes.

Mistress has been entertaining again.

Sigh!

Bath brick

1850: Joel Houghton creates the world's first dishwasher, a hand-cranked device that splashes water onto dishes but fails to clean them.

1885: Eugène Daquin's device has a set of revolving hands that grab the dishes and plunge them into soapy water. It's terrifying!

It'll turn on us next!

1886: Josephine Cochrane invents the first automatic dishwasher. It washes dishes faster than by hand – and without breaking them!

DISHWASHER. A pump draws water into the base of the machine. The detergent dispenser opens, releasing the detergent. A pump then forces the water through rotating spray arms, spraying the dishes. The water drains, and hot air dries the dishes.

Control panel

Door lock

Upper rack

Heating element

Upper spray arm

Lower rack

Drain hose

Lower spray arm

Float valve (controls water level)

Detergent dispenser

You can do it!

To wash dishes by hand: Run hot water into a sink and pour in detergent. Use rubber gloves, and wash dishes from cleanest to dirtiest, using cloth, sponge or (for burned-on food) steel wool.

It's the future, my love!

You just hate washing up!

1924: William Howard Livens invents a small dishwasher for domestic use, with a design much like today's machines.

1950s–2000s: Dishwasher detergents arrive, first as powders (1950s), then liquids (1980s), gels (1990s) and tablets (2000s).

What else is detergent used for?

Dispersing oil spills

AN OIL SPILL can be an environmental catastrophe, killing wildlife and damaging coasts. Oil dispersants, which contain detergents, break up the oil into small droplets, which then sink and disperse.

As well as helping to wash our clothes and dishes, detergents also keep our houses clean. Since the 20th century, a whole range of specialist products have been developed for cleaning different surfaces, including glass, tile, metal, carpets and upholstery. But we don't use detergents only for housework. They can also be found in some quite surprising places…

1. One end of detergent molecule sticks to oil, the other end to water.
2. Wave action helps pull oil apart into ever smaller droplets.
3. Droplets sink to ocean floor, causing less harm.

TOOTHPASTE. Have you ever wondered what causes toothpaste to foam? It's because it contains a mild detergent, which helps to loosen and break down substances on your teeth so they can be dissolved and washed away.

How it works

Silk makers use detergent to get rid of a gum-like substance called sericin that coats silk fibres, making them stick to each other. The silk is dipped in a solution of soda ash and a detergent called Orvus paste, and is soon degummed.

When you've finished, could you give my car a clean?

FIREFIGHTING. Detergents are used to make foams to put out fires. As surfactants, they spread over the surface of the burning material so that oxygen cannot reach it. Without oxygen, a fire cannot continue to burn.

CAR FUEL. Detergents are often added to petrol to prevent the build-up of harmful deposits in car engines. This enables the cars to run more efficiently and with lower carbon emissions.

25

What happens to used soap?

Where do soap and detergent go once we've used them and rinsed the dirty, foamy water down the drain? It all goes through the sewage system to a treatment plant, where the water is cleaned and put back into the environment, hopefully without harming anything.

Actually, detergents in particular used to do quite a lot of harm to the environment. Until the 1970s, detergents were non-biodegradable – in other words, they didn't break down in the environment, and many waterways became clogged with foam. Since then, the industry has developed biodegradable detergents. That's not to say they cause *no* damage, though…

Asthma?

PHOSPHATES are chemicals in detergents that boost the growth of tiny plants called algae. Algae can cover the water surface, killing fish life by reducing oxygen.

SURFACTANTS IN WATER can harm fish, stopping their gills from working. Luckily, modern surfactants break down too quickly to cause major damage.

SURFACTANTS don't stop working once they go down the drain. They continue to combine with oil and water.

Algae

Didn't there use to be a nice lake around here?

You can do it!

We can all help the environment by:
• not washing our clothes too often
• using eco-friendly soaps and detergents
• recycling packaging.

No, it's those wretched surfactants!

BIOLOGICAL DETERGENTS contain chemicals called enzymes that make them better at tackling food stains, sweat and mud.

Enzymes reduce the need for surfactants. This lessens the damage that detergents do to the environment.

ECO-FRIENDLY soaps and detergents use fewer chemical ingredients. They don't include perfumes, colour or brightening agents, which can cause rashes and allergies. They also use less packaging, which is better for the environment.

Do we really need soap?

Yes, we do! By helping to prevent contamination with germs, soap has led to huge improvements in our health and life expectancy. We wouldn't want to return to a time before we used soap and soaplike products to clean ourselves and our homes. Imagine going to a restaurant, knowing that the kitchen hadn't been cleaned with detergent, or that the staff hadn't washed their hands with soap. It's a bit off-putting, isn't it? And yet, is it possible that we overuse soap? Are there other ways of keeping clean?

YOU WOULDN'T want to eat at this revolting restaurant!

1. *Rats and mice.*
2. *Cockroaches.*
3. *Dirty pots and pans encrusted with old food.*
4. *Food preparation surfaces not cleaned.*
5. *Dirty dishcloth.*
6. *Dirty apron.*
7. *Rubber gloves not used when handling raw meat.*
8. *Waiter with cold serving food.*

LIVING WITHOUT SOAP.
Today, some people have decided to live without soap and shampoo, bathing only in warm water (right). They claim that their skin feels and looks better for it, and they don't suffer any body odour.

NATURALLY CLEAN? The no-soapers say skin produces its own natural cleansing oils, as well as useful bacteria. Experts say that washing in soap and warm water wards off infection.

Hand sanitisers are good at killing bacteria, but they don't remove all organic material, and they can cause dry skin. Use them only in the absence of soap and water.

You'll feel even better with this.

ASH OR SAND are sometimes used as alternatives where soap is not available (below). But washing with soap and water is still the best way of staying clean.

Sand's better than nothing.

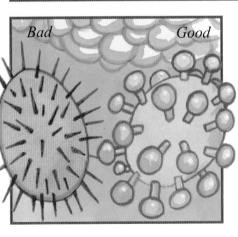

Bad   _Good_

ANTIBACTERIAL SOAPS are popular today, but many experts say they are not that useful. They must be left on the skin for 2 minutes to work; bacteria may build up resistance to them; they kill all bacteria, including the good kind (left); and they don't work against viruses.

Glossary

Alkali A chemical, such as lime or soda, that neutralises an acid.

Ammonia A colourless gas with a pungent smell. It dissolves in water to give a strongly alkaline solution.

Antibacterial soap Soap that contains chemicals that kill bacteria.

Bacteria Single-celled microorganisms, some of which can cause disease.

Carbon emissions The discharge of carbon dioxide into the atmosphere.

Detergent A cleansing agent that combines with dirt to make it more soluble in water. Unlike soap, it does not form a scum in hard water.

Emery powder A greyish-black powder used as an abrasive to polish, smooth or grind metals.

Enzyme A substance produced by a living organism that brings about particular chemical reactions.

Fatty acid A type of naturally occurring acid containing a long chain of carbon atoms.

Fungus A type of organism, including moulds, yeast and mushrooms. Some fungi can cause infections.

Glycerine A colourless, sweet, thick liquid formed during soapmaking.

Hand sanitiser A gel, foam or liquid hand cleanser that contains bacteria-killing chemicals.

Hard water Water that has a high mineral content.

Hydrotherapy The use of exercises in a pool to help treat conditions such as arthritis.

Incense A substance such as a gum or spice, burned for the sweet smell it produces.

Limescale A whitish deposit on the inside of pipes, pots and kettles, caused by minerals from water.

Lye A strongly alkaline solution of, for example, potassium hydroxide, used for washing and cleaning.

Microorganism Any organism that is too small to be seen without a microscope.

Molecule A group of atoms bonded together.

Nausea The feeling of being about to vomit.

Neutralise To make an acidic or alkaline substance chemically neutral.

Ochre A natural pigment that ranges from light yellow to brown or red.

Organism Any living thing.

Protozoa Single-celled microorganisms with animal-like behaviour, including movement. Some can cause disease.

Pumice A light volcanic rock used as an abrasive for removing hard skin.

Saponification The process of turning fats and oils into soap by reaction with an alkali.

Soda ash A popular name for the chemical sodium carbonate, commonly used as an alkali in soapmaking.

Soluble Able to be dissolved, especially in water.

Strigil An instrument with a curved blade used to scrape sweat and dirt from the skin.

Surfactant A substance that reduces the surface tension of a liquid.

Tallow A hard substance made from melted animal fat, used in making candles and soap.

Virus A type of microorganism that can only reproduce inside a host cell.

Washboard A board made of ridged wood, glass or corrugated metal, used when washing clothes as a surface against which to scrub them.

Index

Top clean societies in history

The Romans

The ancient Romans were famous for their baths, which they called *thermae*, and they introduced these to all the provinces of their empire. A trip to the bathhouse was a daily social activity for all Romans, rich or poor.

Medieval Japan

The first public bathhouse in Japan opened in 1266. Bathhouses included steam rooms (*iwaburo*) and hot-water baths (*yuya*) and were extremely popular.

The Aztecs

One Spanish conquistador described the Aztecs of Mexico as being 'very neat and cleanly, bathing every afternoon'. Aztecs bathed regularly in a *temazcal* (steam house). Bathers washed with a mixture of water, soap and grass, and scrubbed themselves with river stones.

The Ottoman Turks

The Turks of the Ottoman Empire (1299–1923) were great patrons of baths, building enormous palatial *hamams* (bathhouses). Like Roman baths, these consisted of a hot room, a warm room and a cold room.

Ancient Egypt

For soap, the Egyptians used a paste containing ash or clay, which was often scented and could be worked into a lather. Queen Cleopatra, reputedly, preferred to bathe in asses' milk. A few baths have been discovered, but most Egyptians washed themselves in the river.

Aleppo soap

Aleppo soap, known in Arabic as *sapun ghar*, takes its name from the ancient Syrian city of Aleppo. The city thrived on trade, and one of its most popular exports was its famous soap.

Ancient method

To this day, the soap is made in the traditional way. Olive oil, water, and lye are boiled together for three days, after which laurel oil is added. Unlike most other soaps, it does not contain animal fat. The finished mixture is poured onto a flat surface to cool, then cut into cubes. These are then stacked in an underground chamber and left to age for six to nine months. The soap starts out green, but during the ageing process the outside turns yellow.

Kind on the skin

Aleppo soap is not only used for washing but is also an excellent moisturiser. It can help to reduce the pain of insect bites and skin allergies. Because of its mildness, it is often used to bathe infants.

Did you know?

The word *soap* comes from the Latin *sapo*, which in turn was probably borrowed from the Germanic word *saipo*.

- The Greek physician Galen recommended soap as a cleansing product in the 2nd century AD.

- During the Napoleonic Wars, at the beginning of the 19th century, the British government raised a great deal of revenue by taxing soap. Some people attempted to avoid the tax by making soap secretly at night.

- Many of the soap bars on sale in shops today are not strictly speaking soap but 'syndet bars', or synthetic detergent bars.

Soap isn't just useful for keeping clean. Rubbing the bottom of saucepans with soap prevents black cooking marks; if a zip gets stuck, you can loosen it by rubbing a soap bar along the teeth; and scented soap packed in luggage can keep your clothes smelling fresh.

- The oldest bathtub yet discovered is in the palace of Knossos on the Mediterranean island of Crete. It dates from about 1500 BC.

- By the 5th century AD, the city of Rome had 900 public bathhouses. The Baths of Caracalla, built in the 3rd century AD, could accommodate up to 1,600 bathers.